Fold a Banana

and 146 other things to do when you're bored

BY JIM ERSKINE AND GEORGE MORAN

CLARKSON N. POTTER, INC., PUBLISHERS, NEW YORK
Distributed by Crown Publishers, Inc.

Copyright © 1978 by James R. Erskine
Illustrations copyright © 1978 by George Moran
All rights reserved. No part of this publication
may be reproduced, stored in a retrieval
system, or transmitted, in any form or by any
means, electronic, mechanical, photocopying,
recording, or otherwise, without the written
permission of the publisher. Inquiries should
be addressed to Clarkson N. Potter, Inc.,
One Park Avenue, New York, N.Y. 10016.

Published simultaneously in Canada by
General Publishing Company Limited

Printed in the United States of America

Designed by Betty Binns

ILLUSTRATED BY GEORGE MORAN

Library of Congress Cataloging in Publication Data

Erskine, Jim.
  Fold a banana.

  1. Creative activities and seat work.
2. Amusements.   3. Games.   I. Title.
GV1201.E77   1978   790.13   78–17804
ISBN 0-517-535033

Fourth Printing, January, 1979

To apartment 8,
because it was necessary
J.E.

What heart can think,
or tongue express,
the harm that groweth
of idleness?
—JOHN HEYWOOD

INTRODUCTION

For countless ages, boredom has been the scourge of mankind. Everyone, yes, *everyone* has at one time or another been afflicted with the problem of having absolutely nothing to do. You are not alone.

To be sure, there are a number of worthwhile pursuits to which some people apply themselves from time to time (bird watching, philanthropy, organic gardening, yoga), but on the whole, the majority of us merely muck around glumly with nothing to do, and boredom takes its toll in frustration, depression, and untold psychological hang-ups.

But no longer!

You hold in your hands the ultimate answer to boredom, the impetus to the creative spirit that resides within us all. Never again will you face the gloom-ridden prospect of having nothing to do.

Simply turn to this book whenever the spectre of boredom looms. You will be amazed and delighted to learn how stimulating, how invigorating, how enjoyable it can be to do nothing in a positive and constructive manner.

So—

To all who plod lethargically through their day to day existence,

To all who find time weighing heavily on their shoulders,

To all who spend entire afternoons staring at walls and listening to old Kate Smith records,

To all in the grip of the ages-old scourge of boredom,

To all of you who have nothing, absolutely nothing, to do,

TAKE HEART.

This book is for you.

Tell your feet a joke.

Throw a tomato into a fan.

Sing the ABC song backward.

Pretend you are a dog.

Dial a prayer and argue with it.

Vacuum the yard.

See how many pieces of bubble gum
you can chew at one time.

Walk in circles.

Grease the doorknobs.

String up a room.

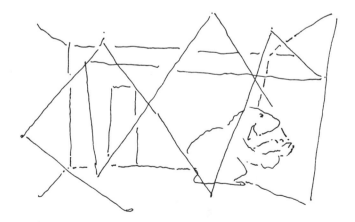

Stack furniture.

Award yourself the Congressional
Medal of Honor.

Relive fond memories.

Tie your shoelaces together.

Take a chair with you
wherever you go.

Gargle.

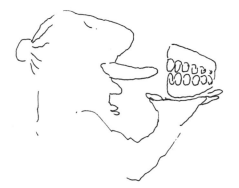

Count your teeth with your tongue.

Whistle "The Star Spangled Banner"
three times, fast.

Decay.

Build a house out of toothpicks.

Howl.

Become a character from your
favorite movie.

Wear a lampshade on your head.

Learn to speak Greek fluently.

Memorize the dictionary.

Stomp grapes in the bathtub.

Find a bug and chase it.

Make yourself a pair of wings.

Strike a pose and say,
"I vant to be alone."

Be immobile.

Dance till you drop.

Check under the chairs
for chewing gum.

Squish a loaf of bread.

Make little dough men out of your
squished bread and eat them.

Moo.

Stack raisins.
Eat the ones that won't stay on top.

Bounce a potato.

Outmaneuver your shadow.

Set your watch back an hour
and live it over.

Stand on your head and pretend
you are walking on the ceiling.

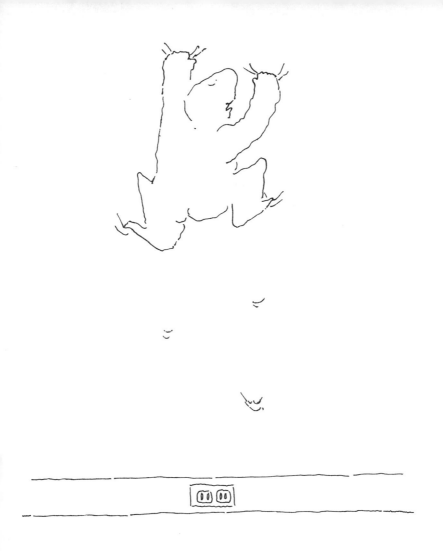

Climb the walls.

EEEEEEE

AAAAH

OOOH

AAAH-HA

AHHHH

OOOoHH

AHHH

Appreciate everything.

Challenge yourself to a duel
(may the best man win).

Believe in Santa Claus.

Throw marshmallows against the wall.

Hold an ice cube as
long as possible.

Make a bunch of paper airplanes
and have an air war.

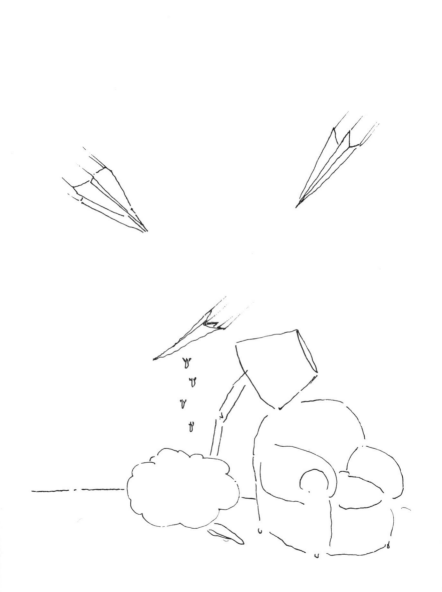

Put on as many shirts, socks,
and pants as you can.

Adopt strange mannerisms.

Blow up a balloon till it pops.

Pretend you are in a restaurant
and complain about the service.

Sing soft and sweet
and clear.

Sing loud and sour
and gravelly.

Open everything.

Balance a pencil on your nose.

Pour milk in your shoes.

Write graffiti under the rug.

Embarrass yourself.

Grind your teeth.

Chew ice.

Turn the radio just a little off station
and see how long you can stand it.

Tie bricks to your shoes
and go for a walk.

Stomp around.

Check for loose change in the sofa.

Paint funny faces on the mirrors.

Lock yourself in a closet and pretend
you are the only one left.

Chase yourself.

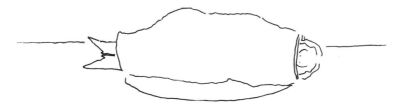

Roll up in a rug.

Dance with a broom.

Wear a paper bag over your head.

Solve a mystery.

Make a mess.

Take a bath with your clothes on.

Smell your sneakers.

Salute the telephone.

Write a book.

Impress yourself.

Sweat.

Shoot rubber bands.

Tie yourself up.

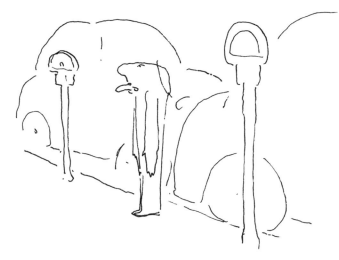

Pretend you are a parking meter.

Fold a banana.

Stick things between your toes.

Act sickeningly cutesy.

Act absurdly macho.

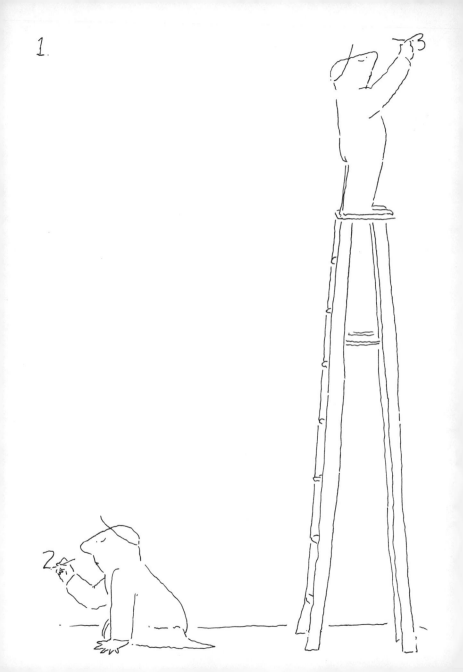

Count all the corners in the house.

Jump on the furniture.

Unplug everything.

Hop to it.

Get dirty.

Creep.

Run up and down the stairs as many
times as you can.

Stuff your pockets.

Count to a million by ones.

Thump your stomach.

Erase all thoughts.

Fight vampires (nighttime only).

Wear your clothes backward.

Crack your knuckles.

Catch a fly.

Make romantic advances to a pillow.

Laugh a jolly old laugh.

Flatter yourself.

Run around the house naked.

Twiddle your thumbs
as long as possible.

Wear your underwear on your head.

Salt your tongue.

Juggle eggs.

Levitate yourself.

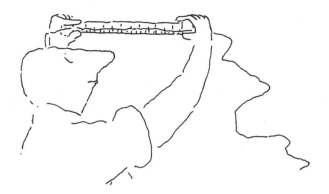

Measure your hair.

Turn everything on.

Play hide-and-seek with a glass of water.

Become paranoid.

Ignore nature's call.

Pound an orange.

Contort your body.

Gift wrap every box in the house.

Tear a phone book in half.

Beat up a pillow.

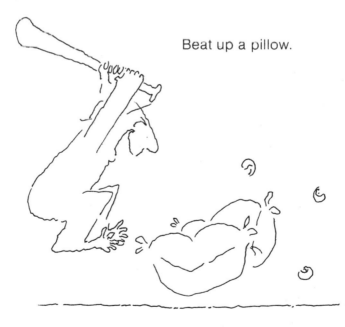

Realize the seriousness
of everything.

Then tell yourself it's all unreal.

Hide from yourself.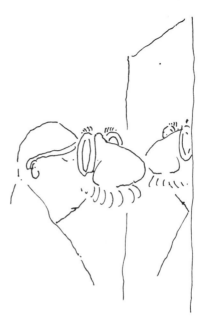

Sweep the ceiling.

Blow bubbles in a glass of milk.

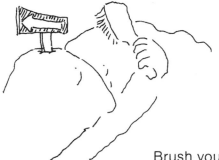

Brush your hair the wrong way.

Run into a wall.

Calculate pi to the last digit.

Touch your nose with your tongue.

Hunt for elves.

Fry your breakfast cereal.

Lower your standards.

Banish evil inclinations.

Pretend you are on a talk show.

Hypnotize yourself.

Say every word you know.

Tape your mouth shut.

Dig for buried treasure.

Get your hand stuck in a jar.

Glue your fingers together.

Take root.

Procrastinate.

Fall.

Spin.

Count all the stars.